PRAYING
the PRAYERS
OF THE
BIBLE
FOR *Kids*

JAMES BANKS
with CINDY KENNEY

Illustrated by
SAM CARBAUGH

Discovery House®
from Our Daily Bread Ministries

For Austin James
Ephesians 1:16
You are loved, always.
–JB

For my parents, with love.
–SC

Praying the Prayers of the Bible for Kids
© 2018 by James Banks
Illustrations by Sam Carbaugh and © 2018 by Our Daily Bread Ministries
All rights reserved.

Discovery House is affiliated with Our Daily Bread Ministries,
Grand Rapids, Michigan.

Requests for permission to quote from this book should be directed to:
Permissions Department, Discovery House, PO Box 3566, Grand Rapids, MI 49501,
or contact us by email at permissionsdept@dhp.org.

Interior design by Kris Nelson/StoryLook Design

Library of Congress Cataloging-in-Publication Data
Names: Banks, James, 1961- author.
Title: Praying the prayers of the Bible for kids / James Banks, with Cindy
Kenney, ; illustrations by Samuel Carbaugh.
Description: Grand Rapids : Discovery House, 2018.
Identifiers: LCCN 2018014715 | ISBN 9781627078993 (pbk.)
Subjects: LCSH: Bible--Prayers--Juvenile literature.
Classification: LCC BS680.P64 B353 2018 | DDC 242/.722--dc23
LC record available at https://lccn.loc.gov/2018014715

Printed in the United States of America
First printing in 2018

CONTENTS

INTRODUCTION
for Parents, Caregivers, and Teachers

The prayers of the Bible are a gift from God. And they're for everyone—old and young alike! Prayer is one of the most significant means of communication we have with the Lord. It is our best opportunity to draw close to Him and develop a relationship.

Praying the Prayers of the Bible for Kids will help you put this gift into the hands of children ages four through eight. The book has been organized into five different themes that represent the kinds of prayers young kids might pray. Each entry begins with a specific prayer taken directly from Scripture, which is followed by a meaningful rhyme that will help children to better understand God, and how to connect and communicate with Him on their level.

Why rhyme? It helps children to remember what they read or hear, and apply what they learn. Rhymes help to promote discovery—and we hope that through this book, children and adults together will discover the joy of communicating with God in prayer!

Encourage children to find a special time of the day to read this book. If you are in class, it might be a wonderful way to begin a session or close your day together. If you are at home, it is often easiest to find some quiet time right before a meal or before going to sleep at night.

May God use this book to richly bless you and the children in your life as you pray!

CHAPTER 1

I Love You, God!

(Prayers of Praise)

Do you ever wonder where everything came from? Who made the animals, the clouds, the trees . . . and people?

The answer is God! He made everything—including you. God is very, very smart. He is very, very strong. And He is very, very loving.

God loves you. And when you love Him back, it makes Him smile. He enjoys it when you talk to Him—that's called "prayer." And when you tell God you love Him, that's called "praise."

Love the LORD your God with all your heart and with all your soul. Love him with all your strength.

DEUTERONOMY 6:5 NIrV

Talking to God
is as easy as talking
to a good friend.
And God wants to
be your very best
friend! He loves
you so much that
He sent His Son,
Jesus, to be a man
on earth. When you
know Jesus, you
know God—and you
will live with Him
forever!

You can talk to God about anything. He just
wants to hear what you're thinking. He will always
listen and do what's best, because God loves you—
no matter what. And you can always say to Him,
"I love you, God!"

Praise the Lord. I will praise the Lord.
I will praise the Lord all my life.
I will sing praise to my God as long as I live.
PSALM 146:1–2 NIrV

I love you, LORD.
You give me strength.

PSALM 18:1 NIrV

You keep me safe. You make me strong.

You help me feel like I belong.

I love you, God. I know you're there—

Listening as I pray this prayer.

I hope I live a life that's long,

Doing right and never wrong.

I want to love you faithfully,

And praise you, God, for loving me!

Know that the LORD is God.
He made us, and we belong to him.

PSALM 100:3 NIrV

*You care for people
and animals alike, O LORD.
How precious is your unfailing love, O God!*

PSALM 36:6–7 NLT

Winter, spring, summer, fall.

The seasons, God—you made them all!

Clouds and rain, ice and snow—

And best of all, a bright rainbow!

Elephants, bears, geese and ducks,

Snakes and frogs and brown woodchucks.

Kangaroos and fish in seas,

Dogs, giraffes, and chimpanzees.

The greenest grass and skies of blue—

God, there's *nothing* you can't do!

*God saw everything he had made.
And it was very good.*

GENESIS 1:31 NIrV

You, LORD, are my God!
I will praise you for doing the wonderful
things you [have] planned and promised.

ISAIAH 25:1 CEV

I'm thankful you are at my side,

Every day to be my guide.

You made the world. You made me, too.

You make me want to shout, "Yahoo!"

What are some things that
make you want to shout, "Yahoo!"?

Praise the Lord, day by day.
God our Savior helps us.

PSALM 68:19 ICB

God, I love to hear your story,

Filled with love and strength and glory.

You show me how much you care,

And when I need you—you are there.

I know that I can trust in you.

You're the One who sees me through!

Name one or two of your
favorite Bible stories.

You are my God,
and I will praise you.

PSALM 118:28 NIrV

You care for me both night and day.

You watch me when I sleep and play.

If I'm in bed and have the flu,

I know that I can count on you.

And when I fall and skin my knee,

You're always there to comfort me.

So even when I don't feel good,

I'll still praise you, like I should!

Can you draw a picture
of God's beautiful creation?

You, LORD, are all I want!
You are my choice, and you keep me safe.

PSALM 16:5 CEV

Sometimes at night when I'm afraid,

I feel better once I've prayed.

Or in the day, if I feel sad,

The thought of you can make me glad.

I know you're watching from above,

Guarding me with perfect love.

The LORD says, "I will save the one who loves me.
I will keep him safe, because he trusts in me."

PSALM 91:14 NIrV

I will be filled with joy because of you.
I will sing praises to your name.

PSALM 9:2 NLT

You are so good—it makes me sing!
I thank you, God, for everything!
I'll shout about the things you do,
And praise you just for being you!

I know you made things big and small—
Lord, I love you for them all!
I want to jump! I want to sing!
For all the joy and fun you bring!

Best of all is the love you give—
In your Son, Jesus, I can live!
And so it's both my hands I raise
To honor you with so much praise!

What has God done
that makes you really happy?

"Praise the Lord,
the God of Israel. . . .
[You have] sent us
a mighty Savior."

LUKE 1:68–69 NLT

Oh, Jesus, I can share with you
The love of all my heart.
I know that you are there for me,
And we will never part.

I want to follow where you lead
And see the things you do.
Because you want to be my friend,
I want to be yours, too!

Dear friends, let us love one another, because love
comes from God. Everyone who loves has become a
child of God and knows God. Anyone who does not
love does not know God, because God is love.
Here is how God showed his love among us.
He sent his one and only Son into the world.
He sent him so we could receive life through him.

1 JOHN 4:7–9 NIrV

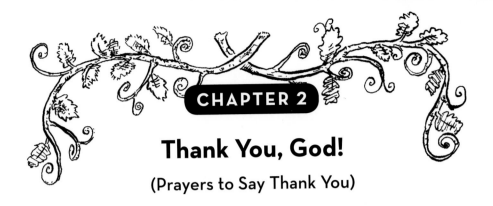

CHAPTER 2

Thank You, God!

(Prayers to Say Thank You)

What do you say when someone does something nice for you?

You say, "Thank you!"

Saying thanks is a great way to tell others that you liked what they did. It makes people smile when they hear "thank you"—and it makes God happy too.

Lots of people do nice things for us all the time. But God does the most. He makes the sun come up every morning. He keeps our hearts beating, gives us food to eat, and helps us through our days. Best of all, He sent Jesus to be our closest friend in the whole world.

Let's thank God for everything He does!

Praise the Lord!
Thank the Lord because he is good.
His love continues forever.
PSALM 106:1 ICB

You thrill me, LORD,
with all you have done for me!

PSALM 92:4 NLT

Some people like to cheer at games
And yell and shout out their team's names.
But God, what I would like to do,
Is yell and shout and cheer for you!
Yeah, God!

You're watching over as I play—
You help me out in every way.
You sent your Son to be my friend
And give me life without an end!

So God, what I would like to do,
Is yell and shout and cheer for you!
Yeah, God!

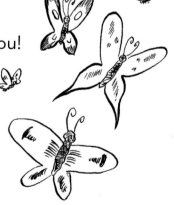

My heart jumps for joy. With my song I praise him.

PSALM 28:7 NIrV

I praise you because of the wonderful way you created me. Everything you do is marvelous!

PSALM 139:14 CEV

All my fingers, all my toes,

Eyes and ears and mouth and nose!

Hands I use to brush my hair,

Legs for leaping through the air!

And for every inside part—

Brains and lungs and bones and heart!

A smile for everyone to see—

Thank you, God, for making me!

I am who I am, it's true—

All because of You-Know-Who!

What are some things you would like to thank God for?

We thank you, O God!
We give thanks because you are near.
People everywhere tell
of your wonderful deeds.

PSALM 75:1 NLT

For planets, stars, the moon and sun,

For time to play and feet to run,

For all the things you've ever done—

God, I give you thanks!

For all the critters in the zoo,

For all my friends, my family too,

For troubles that you see me through—

God, I give you thanks!

For being there when I have cried,

For always staying by my side,

For sending Jesus as my guide—

God, I give you thanks!

God is able to shower all kinds of blessings on you.
So in all things and at all times
you will have everything you need.

2 CORINTHIANS 9:8 NIrV

"Father, thank you for hearing me.
You always hear me."

JOHN 11:41–42 NLT

God, you sent your Son to earth

To show us just how much we're worth.

And when he prayed you always heard—

Every single little word.

He came to help me talk to you,

So I could learn to say thanks too.

Can you say thanks to God
without using words?

It is wonderful to be grateful and to sing your praises, LORD Most High!

PSALM 92:1 CEV

Sometimes I say things I should not.

I fight with friends more than I ought.

But you forgive me when I'm wrong

And teach me how to get along.

And when I am a "Grumpy Gus,"

Or pitch a fit and raise a fuss,

It's better when I think of *you*—

And thank you, Lord, for all you do.

Don't worry about anything. No matter what happens, tell God about everything. Ask and pray, and give thanks to him. Then God's peace will watch over your hearts and your minds. He will do this because you belong to Christ Jesus.

PHILIPPIANS 4:6–7 NIrV

I give you thanks, O LORD,
with all my heart.

PSALM 138:1 NLT

You do more things than I can count—
I cannot count to that amount!
A number that's so very high,
So way up high, it's in the sky!

But still I want to say, "Thank you!"
For each and every thing you do.
So how and where do I begin
To name them all and make you grin?

All I can do is try my best—
Begin each day as I get dressed.
Then say a prayer and name a few
Of all the awesome things you do.

I'll name as many as I can
Throughout the day—yep, that's my plan!
I'll thank you, Lord, and send my love
And know you're listening from above.

Let's count some of the things
God does for you!

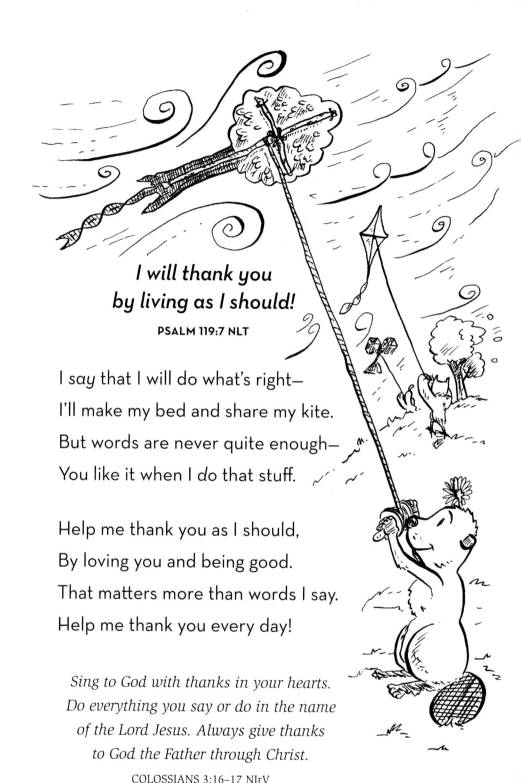

I will thank you by living as I should!

PSALM 119:7 NLT

I say that I will do what's right—
I'll make my bed and share my kite.
But words are never quite enough—
You like it when I do that stuff.

Help me thank you as I should,
By loving you and being good.
That matters more than words I say.
Help me thank you every day!

Sing to God with thanks in your hearts.
Do everything you say or do in the name
of the Lord Jesus. Always give thanks
to God the Father through Christ.

COLOSSIANS 3:16–17 NIrV

CHAPTER 3

I Want to Be Your Friend

(Prayers about Friendship and Faithfulness)

God really loves you. And because He loves you, He wants to be your friend. But not just any friend—He wants to be the best friend you could ever have.

The Bible is filled with stories about how much God loves us, and how we can be friends with Him. It also shows us how to talk to God—even when we have trouble doing what He wants us to. These prayers from the Bible can make us better friends with God and His Son, Jesus.

My heart has heard you say,
"Come and talk with me."
And my heart responds,
"LORD, I am coming."

PSALM 27:8 NLT

There's so much I can tell you, God—
I have a lot to say!
And when I want to talk to you
You never run away!

You love it when I pray to you—
You wait for me to come.
So here I am, let's talk awhile—
'Cause talks with you are fun!

What is your favorite thing
to talk to God about?

Your word is like a lamp that shows me the way. It is like a light that guides me.

PSALM 119:105 NIrV

When it's night, I like some light
To shine so I won't stumble.
If I can see in front of me,
Then I won't take a tumble!

God, your Book can help me see
The things that give me trouble.
Because it's true and shows me you,
I love the Bible *double*!

Jesus . . . said, "I am the light of the world.
If you follow me, you won't have to walk in darkness,
because you will have the light that leads to life."

JOHN 8:12 NLT

Teach me to follow you,
and I will obey your truth.
Always keep me faithful.

PSALM 86:11 CEV

"Follow the Leader" is fun to play,
Dear God, with all the words you say!

The Bible shows me what to do,
And how I can stay close to you.

I will follow where you lead.
Obey your Word? Yes, I've agreed!

Help me read it every day,
And follow closely all the way!

What makes you feel close to Jesus?

*LORD, show me your right way of living,
and make it easy for me to follow.*

PSALM 5:8 ERV

Lord, sometimes it's really hard

To do the things you say.

I know I shouldn't lie or fight,

But rather love and pray.

So when I want to do what's wrong,

I'll stop and say a prayer.

You will help me do what's right

And kind and good and fair!

Did you know that you can tell God
when you want to do something wrong,
and He will help you do what's right?

I praise your promises!

PSALM 56:10 CEV

You've made so many promises,
And all of them are true!
You're perfect and you cannot lie—
The things you say, you'll do!

God, thank you for your promises—
Each one is very good!
Help me find them in your Word
And trust you like I should.

Did you know that God
always keeps His promises?

***You have looked deep into my heart, LORD,
and you know all about me.***

PSALM 139:1 CEV

You know me, God, so very well—
All the secrets I could tell.
You see me when I'm good and bad,
Happy, sneaky, scared, or sad.

There's nothing 'bout me you don't know—
Know it all yet love me so!
You are my friend the whole day through—
I'm glad to have a friend like you!

*God, your thoughts about me are priceless.
No one can possibly add them all up.*

PSALM 139:17 NIrV

Like a lost sheep,
I've gone down the wrong path.
Come and look for me.

PSALM 119:176 NIrV

Dogs and cats will sometimes run
Away from friends and everyone!
When they go and start to roam,
We have to find them—bring them home!

God, we too have run from you
With thoughts we think and things we do.
Many things we know are wrong—
But we still do them all day long.

Jesus, you came after me
To draw me near, so I can be
Close beside you, day and night.
I'll follow you and do what's right.

I am the good shepherd, and the good shepherd
gives up his life for his sheep.

JOHN 10:11 CEV

"I do have faith! Please help me to have even more."

MARK 9:24 CEV

God, I cannot see the wind,
But it still moves my kite.
And I can't always see the stars,
But they still shine at night.

And even though I can't see you,
God, help me trust you're there—
To love you and believe in you
And know you always care.

God says, "Be still and know that I am God."
PSALM 46:10 ICB

Give me a heart that doesn't want anything more than to worship you.

PSALM 86:11 NIrV

I want this, and I want that—
A bicycle, a baseball bat!
A puppy dog, and building blocks,
A swimming pool, and big sandbox!
A dinosaur, a cat that sings—
Oh, I want so many things!

But all that stuff can never fill
A lonely heart—though God you will!
Things may go, but you will stay—
And then be with me every day.
God, you're awesome—yes, it's true!
Help me most to just want you!

Think of a toy that you don't play with anymore—
then thank God that you will never outgrow Him!

I love to do what you say.

PSALM 119:35 CEV

Being bad just makes me sad—
It really isn't fun.
It's like when dark clouds come along
And block out all the sun.

That's when I know it's time to go
To you—and pray and pray!
I need you, Lord, to help me out.
I know you'll show the way!

Doing right is like a light
That shines for many miles.
It makes you happy—and me too!
And then we're *both* all smiles.

Can you think of something
you might say or do to make God smile?

> *"Lord, you know everything.*
> *You know that I love you."*
>
> **JOHN 21:17 NLT**

I thank you, Jesus—you love me!
You know I love you too.
But how I want to love you more
With all I say and do!

The more I am your friend each day,
The more that I will see—
You are the best Friend ever!
You always will love me!

Tell God three things that you love about Him!

CHAPTER 4

I Need Your Help

(Prayers about Daily Needs)

We all need food to eat, water to drink, and clothes to wear. We need a place to live and someone to love and take care of us.

God gives us all of these things because He loves us and is good to us. And because He is, there is something we need more than anything else. Do you know what that is?

It's God himself! If God gives us everything we need, then what we need most is Him! We get to know God better through His Son, Jesus, by reading His Word, the Bible, and by praying to Him. He wants us to ask Him for anything we need. God wants us to depend on Him to always take care of us.

"Don't worry and say, 'What will we eat?' or 'What will we drink?' or 'What will we wear?' That's what those people who don't know God are always thinking about. Don't worry, because your Father in heaven knows that you need all these things. What you should want most is God's kingdom and doing what he wants you to do. Then he will give you all these other things you need."
MATTHEW 6:31–33 ERV

"Give us today our daily bread."

MATTHEW 6:11 NIrV

Peanut butter, hot dogs, and caramel apple pie,
Chicken wings and pizza, and pancakes piled high!
Warm gooey cookies and marshmallow fluff—
Many yummy things to eat—I cannot get enough!

Warm fuzzy jammies and a bed to snuggle in,
Lots of toys to play with and a puppy I call Flynn,
A family who loves me and friends who come to play—
Lord, you care for all my needs, every single day!

God, I want to thank you for all the things you give.
You even shared your perfect Son,
To show us how to live.
I never will forget, Lord, how much you really care.
Now help me to remember that
you taught us how to share!

What do you have
that you can share with others?

You know when I sit down or stand up.
You know my thoughts even when I'm far away.
You see me when I travel and when
I rest at home. You know everything I do.

PSALM 139:2–3 NLT

God, you're always watching—
You know everything I do.
When I sit down or I stand up,
You even know that too!

You're so faithful, Jesus!
You are with me all the way!
Please help me trust that you are there
And love you more each day.

Nothing in all creation can separate us
from God's love for us in Christ Jesus our Lord!

ROMANS 8:39 CEV

*Keep us from being tempted
and protect us from evil.*

MATTHEW 6:13 CEV

How I need your help, Lord,

With choices that I make.

You gave us rules to follow—

Rules I don't want to break!

Every day I'm tempted with things I shouldn't do,

So when I am please

Give me strength to always follow you.

Whenever I do something that

You've told me not to do,

It makes me feel so very sad—

And makes you feel sad too!

God, because I love you, I want to do what's right.

Please help me choose your way,

Jesus, every day and night!

What sort of things tempt you to do wrong?
How can you remember to follow God instead?

*Forgive us for doing wrong,
as we forgive others.*

MATTHEW 6:12 CEV

God, sometimes I do the things that I shouldn't.

I know they are wrong, and I thought that I
 wouldn't!

I'll tell you "I'm sorry"—it's what I must do!

And you will forgive me and say, "*I love you.*"

When others hurt me, or make me feel bad,

It can be hard and sometimes I get mad—

But then it's *my* turn to show love and forgive,

Like you did for me! That's how I will live!

When do you find it hard to say,
"I'm sorry"?
How does it feel when someone forgives you?

**I can lie down and sleep soundly
because you, LORD, will keep me safe.**

PSALM 4:8 CEV

I go to bed and sleep each night
So thankful that you're near.
I'm not afraid if things go *bump*,
Because you're always here!

I like that you watch over me.
You keep me safe and warm.
I'll smile wide and snuggle down,
Within the dark or storm!

God gives rest to his loved ones.

PSALM 127:2 NLT

"You have the power to make me well."

MARK 1:40 CEV

I stub my toe. I scrape my knee.
My tummy ache is hurting me.
My broken leg is not okay.
My ear—it aches! Oh, what a day!

I'm wheezing, sneezing, quite a mess.
I wish my rash would itch me less!
I wonder why am I so ill.
But then I think—*you love me still!*

Your love's so BIG! You always care.
You're always listening for my prayer.
I know that you will calm my fears.
You're right beside me through my tears.

Can you think of a time that you were sick
and God took care of you?

*[I] always pray that God will show [me]
everything he wants [me] to do and
that [I] may have all the wisdom
and understanding that his Spirit gives.*

COLOSSIANS 1:9 CEV

When I need to make a choice
And don't know what to do,
I ask you for answers, Lord—
And you will help me through!

I ask you for your wisdom—
There's so much I don't know.
God, will you please show the way—
The way that I should go?

Who does God use to help you make good choices?

*Trust the Lord with all your heart.
Don't depend on your own understanding.
Remember the Lord in everything you do.
And he will give you success.
Don't depend on your own wisdom.
Respect the Lord and refuse to do wrong.
Then your body will be healthy.
And your bones will be strong.*

PROVERBS 3:5–8 ICB

I treasure your word above all else;
it keeps me from sinning against you.

PSALM 119:11 CEV

The Bible is your Word, God—
    the perfect book to read.
You gave it so that I can grow
    and learn just what I need.

So when I'm seeking answers
    (and do not have a clue),
I'll read your Word so you can show me
    just what I should do.

The Bible teaches love and truth.
    It shows me what things mean.
It's filled with people just like me
    and many things unseen!

The Bible tells of Jesus—
    your Son sent from above.
His life was an example of
    the way we all should love.

Teach me from your Word, God.
    Show me where to start.
Help me learn to love your Word
    and hold it in my heart.

Choose one of your favorite stories from the
Bible and tell it to someone you know!

LORD, show me your ways.
Teach me how to follow you.
Guide me in your truth. Teach me.
You are God my Savior.
I put my hope in you all day long.

PSALM 25:4–5 NIrV

Lord, I love to think of you,

So thankful you are near.

You meet my needs and guide my steps—

You make my pathway clear.

You help me when there's trouble,

Or when I'm feeling scared.

I read your Word, so I can learn

And always be prepared.

Please help me show your love, Lord,

To everyone I know

And let me share how good you are,

Everywhere I go.

Who would you like to share
God's love with today?

*I pray that Christ will live in your hearts
because of your faith. . . .
Christ's love is greater than
any person can ever know.
But I pray that you will be able to
know that love. Then you can be
filled with the fullness of God.*

EPHESIANS 3:17–19 ICB

There's no one like you, Jesus!
Yes, you're the one for me!
I want your love to fill me up
So everyone can see.

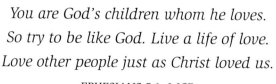

I want to learn to love like you
In everything I do.
Then all my friends can see and know
Your love is for *them* too!

*You are God's children whom he loves.
So try to be like God. Live a life of love.
Love other people just as Christ loved us.*

EPHESIANS 5:1–2 ICB

CHAPTER 5

God Bless You!

(Prayers about Blessings)

God bless you!" Sometimes we say that when people sneeze—it's a nice way of telling them we want God to help them to feel better.

But what is a blessing? A blessing is something good that God does for us. When we pray for blessings, we're asking God for good things—and God wants us to ask! God loves to bless us, and He loves it when we ask Him to bless others!

Sometimes when we ask God to bless us, He doesn't give us what we ask for—or He may not give us what we want right away. But that doesn't mean God isn't listening. God is always listening, and He always cares. It simply means that God knows what is best for us, and He wants us to trust Him to know that. So God's blessings come if and when He knows they will be best for us!

Did you know that we can also bless God? It's true! We can tell God that we love Him, and we can tell others how wonderful and loving He is. Blessing God is another way of praising Him.

In this part of the book, we are going to ask God to bless us, and to bless others too. We're also going to praise God by telling Him how amazing He is. It's fun to pray about blessings!

May God bless *you* as you pray!

With all my heart I want your blessings.

PSALM 119:58 NLT

I really want your blessings, God.

There's nothing I want more!

Because you always give good things,

You're better than a store!

But it's not just about the stuff—

A toy or bike or ball—

There's no blessing as good as *you*.

I want you most of all!

Why is God better than
anything in the whole world?

"Be with me so I will be safe from harm."

1 CHRONICLES 4:10 CEV

Please keep me safe! I need you so
On sidewalks, sand, and in the snow.
Please shield me from mean dogs that bite,
And bullies who just want to fight.

Please help me, God, to not get hurt,
If I do "face-plants" in the dirt!
And when I'm scared of anything
I'll think of you—my Lord and King!

At what times do you especially
want God to keep you safe?

"Every good thing I have is a gift from you."

PSALM 16:2 CEV

Every single thing that's mine—
Stuff I play with all the time—
Fun things, good things, old and new,
Each one is a gift from you.

Thank you, Lord, because you give
Everything I need to live.
Help me always know it's true—
Every blessing comes from you!

What blessings do you have
that you would like to thank God for?

"I pray that you will let me see you in all of your glory."

EXODUS 33:18 CEV

I like superheroes

And all the things they do.

But, God, there's not a single one

Who can compare to you!

Jesus, you're amazing!

I pray that I will see

You in all your awesomeness

When you come back for me!

What would you like to say to Jesus
when you see Him face-to-face?

I pray that the Lord Jesus Christ
will bless you and be kind to you!
May God bless you with his love.

2 CORINTHIANS 13:13 CEV

When other people pray for me,

It makes me feel so good!

Please help me pray for my friends too,

And love them like I should!

I ask you, Lord, to bless my friends,

And bless my family too.

May everybody know your love—

There is no friend like you!

Name three people you would like
God to bless, and say why!

> ### *"I pray that the LORD will bless and protect you."*
>
> **NUMBERS 6:24 CEV**

You always keep me safe, dear Lord.
Please guard my loved ones too.
You're stronger than a castle!
It's good to trust in you!

Take care of them, like you do me,
And keep them from all harms.
God, may they always want to be
Safe in your mighty arms!

Who would you like God
to take care of and keep safe?

LORD, may glory be given to you, not to us. You are loving and faithful.

PSALM 115:1 NIrV

Anything that's good in me
Is all because of *you*.
All good things come from your hands—
It's something that you do!

Please help me to be humble,
To love you like I should.
And give you all the glory—
Because you are so good!

Every good and perfect gift is from God.

JAMES 1:17 NIrV